Investing for Beginners

Investing for Beginners 2 and Bitcoin 1

By Sam Sutton and Stephen Smith

Investing for Beginners:

The Only Money Guide You'll Ever Need

By Sam Sutton

TABLE OF CONTENT

Bitcoin

Introduction

Congratulations, and thank you for purchasing *Investing for Beginners: The Only Money Guide You'll Ever Need.*

Once upon a time, getting into the world of investing was only possible if you were incredibly wealthy, or if you knew someone who could help you. Otherwise, investing was pretty much ignored by many. In fact, a great deal of the population actually feared the idea of investing, as they were concerned that they may lose all of their money.

The reality of investing has changed significantly in the past several years. Nowadays, people who don't invest are almost certainly doomed to have a poor relationship with money. Those who do not take the time to learn how they can effectively invest are essentially putting themselves directly at risk of inflation, which is an inevitable experience of our modern world.

Fortunately, you do not have to be incredibly wealthy or have a friend with the right know-how to get involved in investing. Instead, you simply need to have a sum of money to get started with, nearly any sum will do, and you must also have the desire to learn. Through this book, I am going to teach you the many ways that you can get started with investing and how you can begin to make your money work for you.

Throughout each chapter, you will learn to understand why investing is so important, how it can help you increase your income, the primary things that you need to know about investing, and which investment strategies are the best for you. By the end, you should be feeling confident in your ability to produce a wonderful investment portfolio that will serve you for years to come.

If you are ready to tap into a wonderful money-making opportunity that was once only reserved for the elite few, then this book is the perfect read for you. I hope that you are able to learn plenty from it and that by the end you feel confident in your ability to build your investments wisely, strategically, and successfully. Please, enjoy your read and be sure to follow the tips provided so you can get the most from this book!

Did you know that a large percent of people who make a lot of money lose it within the first couple years?

It doesn't take much for a person to lose all of their money. Around 2 in 3 lottery winners lose all of their winnings within 5 years. If someone could lose hundreds of millions of dollars over a couple years, how fast will you lose your millions that you could make from this book?

Over the past couple years I have stumbled upon the key secret behind managing money and KEEPING it. If you follow the link below you will uncover the truth behind managing and keeping the money you make

>>> Click/Tap here to Learn the Secret Behind Money Management

<<<

Or Go to https://secretstomoneymanagement.gr8.com/

Chapter 1: Benefits of Investing

Investing has many wonderful benefits behind it. The primary benefit is that you will increase your savings so that you have more money in the long-term. However, this is not the only benefit that you will reap from investing! Let's explore what the many benefits of investing include.

Long-Term Returns

One of the biggest benefits of investing is that you increase your potential for long-term returns on your investments. For example, if you invest in a stock market and ride it out, in a few years' time the stock increases significantly, you then increase the amount of money you have. This is typically the biggest reason why people begin investing in the first place. The idea of being able to invest whatever amount you have available in something that will essentially sit there and increase the value of your funds over time is exciting. Knowing that your money is not simply sitting there and being stagnant, but rather it is actively growing on its own means that you can feel confident that you are taking active and effective measures toward your financial growth in the long run.

Don't Suffer From Inflation

One of the problems with simply keeping your funds in a savings account is that it does not rise with inflation. If you have your money sitting in a savings account, the purchasing power of your money significantly decreases over time. That is because you have the same amount of money, but the value of goods is always increasing. Essentially, this is no longer an effective way to hedge yourself against inflation and ensure that you have a healthy 'nest egg' anymore. At one time, savings accounts were powerful and people did not need to worry about purchasing power or inflation. However, that age has long since passed. Inflation is a very real risk and it regularly becomes an issue for virtually anyone who has not taken the time to invest.

If you invest your money effectively and properly, the value of your money increases as the value of commodities increase. This means that your money is inflating alongside the active market. As a result, you know that your purchasing power will remain strong. You will always know that the money you have set aside is plenty enough to cover the rising costs of goods. Rather than worrying that inflation will cripple you, you will know that you are actively and smartly working with the market alongside inflation, rather than slowly drowning beneath it.

Creating a Residual Income Source

Investing is a wonderful way to create a source of residual income. The profits you earn from your investments are gained through very minimal work on your behalf, depending on the types of investments you have chosen to make. Some of these may not be accessible for some time, though other forms of investments are accessible immediately. For example, if you invest in real estate. Not only is the property itself inflating in value over time, but you can also rent out the property and earn monthly income from the property.

Residual income is a wonderful way to boost your monthly and annual salaries to ensure that you will always remain in a financially strong position. In modern times, residual income truly is the best way to protect yourself and ensure that you always have plenty of money to use and invest at any given time. This means that should your linear income (money earned directly for your work or invested) ever be reduced, or even be taken away for some period of time, you still have some level of income available to you so that you can maintain your lifestyle.

Invest Based on Your Needs and Abilities

Investing in the modern world truly gives you a wide variety of options to invest in based on your needs, as well as your abilities. This means that investing has become something that is so simple virtually anyone can get involved with it. You no longer have to fit specific criteria so you can invest. Instead, you simply have to be ready to learn how and be willing to take the leap.

Regardless of where you are at, moneywise, investing allows you to consider what you want to gain from your investments and how you can gain that specifically. This means that you can easily choose what you desire: increased profits, protecting your purchasing power, residual income, etc. and then use that as your primary objective when investing. This means that you can gain virtually any financial benefit from your investment.

The fact that you can invest based on your unique abilities is also important. This means that no matter how much money you have per month or year to invest, you can still get started. Given the many different ways that investing can take place these days, there are no longer strict and large requirements in place before you can get started. The minimum buy-in value ranges, with many investment funds being made available at nominally low prices so that virtually anyone can become involved with investing.

Little to No Action Required

Depending on what you plan to invest in and how much of your time you want to invest in it, investing can take little to no required action to get your desired results. Instead, you can easily choose strategies that require absolutely no time at all. Or, alternatively, you can choose ones that require you to be involved and allow you to keep yourself directly in the line of action with your own investments.

Some examples of choices that allow you to refrain from becoming overly involved include investments made available to you through your bank, mutual funds, and cryptocurrencies. These are ones that can typically be left alone for quite some time. On the other hand, investments that can take more of your time, (unless you choose to hire a manager to overlook your investments) include stocks, real estate, and other commodities.

Prevent Temptation

If your money was already invested, this makes it significantly easier to prevent yourself from being tempted to use it. Many people see funds building in their savings accounts and have a tendency to encourage themselves to dip into it 'just this once.' This can become almost addicting, and before they even know it, they're right back where they started. This can be a major and frustrating cycle for many people. Putting a fair portion of that savings into investments where they can be held long-term makes it much easier for you to ensure that you don't give in to temptation and draw on your savings since they are already allocated and are more difficult for you to access.

As you can see, there are many benefits for people who want to get involved in investing! If you are ready to or are interested in reaping all of these wonderful rewards, you know that investing is for you. Truly, there are no downsides to investing. Nowadays, with how easy it is for people to become involved and the number of benefits that you stand to gain when you do, it is a no-brainer as to why you need to start investing as soon as possible.

Chapter 2: Choosing Your Investment Strategy

Now that you understand how important it is that you begin investing, and the many benefits you stand to gain as a result, you are likely wondering how you're supposed to go about it. There are many strategies for investing, so it is important that you choose the one that works for you. Before we begin diving too deep into the strategies themselves, let's take some time to explore what you need to know so that you can discover which strategy is the best for you. This chapter will help you set your goals clearly and assist you in exploring the options available to you based on those goals.

How to Choose the Strategy That You Need

Choosing the strategy that you need to get the most out of your investments starts with understanding what you actually want to get out of them. Once you are clear on what your goals are, you can begin to understand what types of investment strategies might fit in with your goals. Each investment strategy has a unique opportunity, outcome, and financial requirement. Knowing that the one you picked should perfectly fit several of your own unique needs and requirements can help successfully fulfill your goals.

The following sections will help you set clear goals, understand how much work you are willing to put into your investments, recognizing the benefits of unique investment types, and understanding where you should start. Know that this may seem a little bit overwhelming at first, but it is actually quite simple. Once you understand what you are doing and where you want to start, it becomes a lot easier. We will also discuss your portfolio in the next chapter so that you can get a better understanding of how to create a long-term plan, in addition to an idea of where you should start.

Know What You Desire to Get Out of Your Investments

Understanding what you want to get out of your investments is important. This is essentially where you get to build your investment goals. Here, you get the opportunity to decide what it is that you are most focused on when it comes to your investments. You can also discover your secondary goals, and any other goals you may have. In general, there are four goals that exist when people make investments: short-term growth, long-term growth, residual income, and personal financial asset protection. We will explore each of these goals so that you can understand what they are and why they're relevant. In general, most people have at least 2 or 3, if not all of these goals with their funds. Right now, we want to focus on your primary goals. Once you have discovered those, you can begin making your earliest moves to support your primary goals. Then, as you diversify your portfolio you can begin to focus on your secondary goals.

Short-Term Growth

When your goals are focused on the short-term, this typically means that you have something that you want or need to use the funds for within a year or less. In some cases, it can be as long as 18 months. However, the standard time for short-term investments is about 12 months in length, if not less. Using short-term investment strategies means that you can easily access your funds after that short period of time for whatever you desire to use it for. For example, if you know you want to go on a major trip next summer, want to buy a new car, or do anything else that requires a significant chunk of money but can be completed in a shorter time frame, using short-term investments is the best way to go.

Many people, if not all, have some type of short-term investment strategy in place. This strategy requires a little more time and commitment, as you do have to regularly go in and revisit your strategy and reinforce it after it has reached fruition. However, this is not typically a big deal.

The best way to determine if your goal classifies as a short-term goal is to ask yourself: "Will I need these funds in 12 months or less?" If you will, you know that your primary goal is to have access to your funds soon, meaning that you want to have a short-term investment strategy in place. Doing this may seem ineffective, but the reality is that it is highly beneficial. Using short-term investment strategies means that you can protect your funds against inflation while you save them up. This is more effective than merely keeping the funds in a savings account.

Long-Term Growth

Long-term growth goals are ones that are typically effective after a period of 2 years or longer. The average term ranges from 5-10 years, or above 25 years. You often see people using long-term growth solutions to help them save for retirement or for other far-off life experiences. These funds are also great for anyone who may not have any particular goal with their funds but know that they do want to keep them in a protected space. This means that their future-funds can be protected against inflation better than if they were simply stored in a standard savings account.

Long-term growth tends to be the second primary goal for many people. In general, most people want some form of short-term financial investment that they can use quickly, and some form of long-term investment that they can use to protect their future selves against inflation, as well as to save for future events. This may include things such as college for their children as well. The long-term savings are not always intended solely for the individual, as sometimes it is used for future generations instead.

The best way to determine if a long-term investment strategy is the best for you is to ask yourself: "Will I need these funds in the next 2 years?"

If not, you can likely put them straight into a long-term investment fund. This will ensure that they are stashed away, protected against inflation, and working for you.

Residual Income

If your goal is to increase your earning potential and maximize your monthly and annual profits, you want an investment strategy that has a residual income benefit. Technically, any investment strategy that increases the funds you have available to you through profits can be considered residual income. For the purpose of this goal, we are talking about an investment that can be maintained while it provides you with regular profits in the meantime.

The best way to open yourself up to this type of residual income is to begin investing in things such as real estate. When you invest in real estate, in particular, your profits are immediate as well as long-term, depending on how much you invest. In order to create this duality in your investment, you want to purchase a piece of real estate where you would receive income through monthly rental fees. This means that you will be receiving continuous payments from your investment, in addition to having the value of the property itself reserved as a long-term investment.

Personal Financial Asset Protection

Many people do not realize that having insurance is also a form of investment. Although you do not necessarily stand to gain money from insurance, having it in place does protect you against potential losses. As such, it can be considered an investment. In addition to having insurance, another way that you can protect your financial assets is to diversify your portfolio. As you will learn shortly, this is not something you should do right away. Instead, you should aim to focus on one area and then grow from there. However, if you know this is a primary goal for you, then growth would be something that you should focus on incorporating into your strategy early, rather than waiting longer like some other investors tend to do.

Defining Your Goals

The best way to make sure that you are clear on your goals is to look deeply and understand exactly what your goals are. Sit honestly with yourself and explore what it is that you desire to achieve from your investments. Then, you can easily begin to discover what matters most to you. If you feel that you are drawn toward all four main goals, or that you have additional ones that have not been listed, pay attention to ordering them in terms of priority.

Once you have discovered what your goals are and what your priorities are, you will have a better idea of where to start and what to focus on when it comes to investing. This will ensure that any move you make is directly in alignment with your goal, rather than pursuing it because someone else told you it was a good idea. Remember, at the end of the day the funds being invested are yours and you get the final say on what is right for you. The best way you can confidently make that decision is to educate yourself on the facts that go into it, just like you are doing right now!

Be Realistic About How Much Work You Are Willing to Do

Now that you understand what your goals are, you can begin to discover what you are willing to do to actually make them happen. For example, if your goal is to create residual income, but you do not want to be directly involved in the rental market, you might consider that this would be a goal for the future, and maybe not necessarily a primary goal. Alternatively, if you have the funds available to you, you may instead choose to get involved and hire a management team to take over. While this would cut into your profitability, it would also reduce the amount of work required from you when it comes to your investments.

Based on the above scenario, it is clear that you need to understand how much time you are willing to invest into your financial goals, and how much funds you have available to you if the time you need to invest is not worthwhile for you or possible for you at this moment. If the time you have to invest seems too much, you should consider starting with a different goal. For example, investing in mutual funds or the stock market.

Once you are clear on the amount of time you have to invest, you have to make sure that you do not waste any investments by getting involved in something that you do not actually have the time to see through. Fortunately, most investment opportunities are fairly easy to deal with in terms of time. Most do not require you to invest too much time. The least-involved investment strategies include you hiring a portfolio manager and meeting with your manager once per quarter to ensure that your goals are being met and that you update any information as you see fit. So, understand that even if you don't have a large amount of time to invest in your investing strategies, you do still have many offers available to you.

Understanding the Minimum Entry Requirements

In addition to investing time, you also need to think of how much money you can invest. Every strategy you look at will have a minimum entry requirement for you before you can get started. While investing is no longer reserved for those who are particularly wealthy, you still need to have a sufficient amount of funds to start out with. Assess what you have available to you immediately and make your earliest decisions based on that. Once you begin to grow your funds, you can then begin to diversify your portfolio and include those more costly investments that have a higher buy-in value.

Picking Your Starting Point

Now that you are clear on what your goal is, the time required by different investments, and the number of funds you have available to get started with, you should have a fairly clear idea of what your 'launch point' or starting point is for investing. If you have looked over these three things and realize they don't match up, for example, you don't have much time or funds to invest, but you want to get started in real estate or something similar that will offer residual income, ideally you should be choosing a secondary goal that is more accessible to you at the moment. Then, once you reach that goal you can use the funds to go ahead and get started in real estate.

It is important that these three values: your goal, your time, and your startup funds, are in alignment. If for whatever reason they are not, there's a chance your investments might fail. This is because at least one aspect will be out of place and therefore your investment may simply not be affordable, may not work out, or maybe too much for you to effectively handle. For this reason, make sure you start somewhere that is tangible and manageable for you at the moment. Understand that the entire point of getting started in investing is for you to increase your funds, so you can always go ahead and move toward your other primary or secondary goals later on once they become more feasible with your financial standing.

A Note on Starting Out: Choose One to Start

Before we move on, I want to point out one very important thing: when you choose a starting point, choose only one. Too many people make the mistake of going into an investor's office or otherwise and expecting to start out with several different investment funds all at the same time. Unfortunately, many investors will actually agree with this and go ahead with it because they want to offer you the service you are looking for, and they typically make money from it. For you, however, this can be overwhelming and can result in you not getting your needs met.

If you are just starting out, chances are you have not yet found an investor to work with that can understand your needs, works in the way that best suits you, and complements your personality. If you are not working with an investor but instead are going solo, this becomes even more important.

When you are starting out, only start with a single strategy. Just one type of investment. Doing this will ensure that you master that style before moving forward. The same goes for if you are going to an investor. Make sure that you take some time to understand the important concepts, get into the swing of things, understand your investor, and make sure that the entire process runs smoothly before adding anything else to the portfolio. Investing, when done properly, runs like a well-oiled machine. There is no need to waste your time jumping in feet first, getting confused, and potentially making fatal mistakes that deter you from achieving success. Instead, start small with a single focus and grow out from there, one at a time.

Chapter 3: Understanding Your Investment Portfolio

Now that you know your goals and desires, it is time for you to understand your investment portfolio! In this chapter, we are going to cover the basics of your portfolio. This will help ensure that you know what a portfolio is, why it matters, what it looks like, what your goals with your portfolio are, and how you will manage your portfolio.

Your Portfolio Accounts for All of Your Investments

Put simply, your portfolio is the sum of all of your current investments. Whenever you invest in something, it goes into your portfolio. If created properly, your portfolio should clearly reflect your investment goals. For example, if your goal is primarily focused on long-term growth, all of the items within your portfolio should easily identify that and prove it through the investments that are stored within it.

Each time you add a new form of investment to your account, you are adding it to your portfolio. Your portfolio takes the sum of everything and shows yourself, as well as investors, what you are doing with your money and what your focuses are. You can easily look into your portfolio and see if you are successfully and efficiently managing your funds, or if they are not being invested in your best interests. Early on, you may find that it is difficult for you to successfully do it all on your own. This is why it is beneficial to start with just one single investment type in the beginning and move out one at a time. You may find that an investor can help you easily ensure that your portfolio is being managed in the most effective way possible, thus ensuring that you are getting the most out of your funds in a way that easily fuels your goals, rather than hinders your ability to reach them.

What It Means to Diversify Your Portfolio

Diversifying your portfolio essentially means that you are adding new strategies to it. For example, if you started out with something simple like mutual funds and then decided that you wanted to invest in stocks, you are already diversifying your portfolio.

There are two ways that your portfolio can be diversified: investing in new accounts with the same strategy (for example, investing in different types of mutual fund, purchasing real estate in a different city or country, etc.) or, by investing in a new strategy entirely. Typically, you want to start by diversifying within a single strategy before you move on to adding a new one altogether. However, that also depends entirely on what your goals are.

When it comes to the stock market, diversifying is unique. Let's focus on this for a moment so that, should you choose to include the stocks in your portfolio, you will understand what diversifying them means. Essentially, diversifying means investing in many different businesses or commodities so that if one falls or crashes, you are hedged by the others. In every case, you are still invested in the stocks. However, by diversifying who and what you have invested in, you have made it easier for yourself to maximize your income and minimize your risk.

Should You Manage Your Own Portfolio?

Ideally, you should be directly involved in managing your own portfolio. However, you may choose to include an investor in the management as well if you want to make it efficient and less time-consuming. Additionally, including a professional investor means that you are less at-risk of having your investments fall flat or result in you taking a loss of some form. Since investors are highly trained in investing and have a clearer idea of how they can maximize your income and minimize your risk, having a professional on-board is typically a great idea.

It is important to understand, still, what different investment types are and what they mean, however. You want to make sure that if you do choose to hire an investor, you choose one who is acting in your best interest. The best way to make sure of this is to arm yourself with knowledge so that you have a greater understanding of what your investor is talking about, what they are offering you, what they are doing with your funds, and what they should be doing. This is how you can ensure that their actions will benefit you and will focus on the goals you have in mind.

Chapter 4: Banking on Inflation

Banking on inflation essentially means that you are banking on a commodity that is known to match market inflation effortlessly. While this is true for virtually all investment styles, those classified in this specific category tend to be ones that are easier for you to invest in on your own, without the help of an investor or a banker's assistance. In this chapter, you are going to learn about how you can bank on inflation yourself, through three primary strategies.

Types of Strategies that Bank on Inflation

There are three primary strategies that allow you to bank on inflation on your own, without requiring the assistance of an investor or a banker directly overseeing your investments for you. They include real estate, precious goods, and currency. When you choose to invest in these three strategies with the intention of banking on inflation, your goal is to essentially buy low and sell high. In many cases, you will end up holding on to the commodity for years before you end up selling it. This means that it has typically endured a high amount of inflation and has given you the opportunity to maximize your gains.

If you are someone who has the desire to use investments so you can pass on your wealth to future generations in your family, then you may be particularly inspired to invest in this field. Things such as real estate and precious goods can easily be passed down to future generations so that they can then overlook the investment and, if they see fit, sell it to maximize their profits as well. Let's begin exploring each individual investment option and why they are such a benefit to you as an investor!

Real Estate

Real estate is a great all-around investment for those who can afford it. When you invest in real estate, it provides you the opportunity to create residual income, in addition to long-term growth. Real estate does have a high buy-in value, but there are some ways that you can overcome this. For example, purchasing real estate with a partner or a group of people as opposed to doing it alone. This would allow you to buy a share of the property, rather than buying it outright yourself. If you would prefer to own real estate personally, doing this can initially allow you to raise the capital to go ahead and do it yourself in the future.

When you invest in real estate, you hedge yourself against many different types of financial risks. For example, inflation. When you purchase real estate when the market is low (or in a state that is regularly called a 'buyer's market') you provide yourself with the perfect opportunity to gain possession over something that can earn you an incredible profit. Whether you choose to immediately sell it once the market swings back in the other direction, or hold on to it for many years and earn rental income from it, you can make a great deal of money through real estate.

You should know that there are two ways that real estate can become an investment: through flipping properties, or through buying and renting real estate. When you 'flip' properties, you essentially purchase old run down properties, rebuild or renovate the property, and then sell it as fast as you can. Typically, the shorter amount of time that the house is in your possession, the better. Alternatively, if you are buying a house to rent it out, you want to keep it in your possession for as long as possible. It then becomes an investment in two ways: through residual income, and through long-term growth profits.

In both cases, you do not necessarily have to be heavily involved in the process if you do not want to be. You can easily hire a team to overlook the work and ensure that you stay hands-off as much as possible. Then, your only involvement would be to locate homes, purchase them at exactly the right time, and then turn them over to your team. They would then become responsible for overseeing all of the work done to ensure that it is either flipped in a short period of time or maintained over a long period of time with renters in the house at all times.

Although hiring a team does cut into your profitability, it also gives you plenty of freedom since you have someone to delegate most of the tasks to. If, however, this does not matter to you, then you can certainly be more hands-on. For example, being directly involved in the flipping process, or being directly involved with your renters and overseeing the landlord duties that are required to maintain your property.

A 'final property management' circumstance arises when you are investing in a group. In this situation, the group usually decides on what to do and will often hire a management team to overlook the day-to-day needs of handling the property. At this point, your job is only to cut a check for the group and have the manager overlooking the entire investment keep you updated on the property.

Real estate truly is an incredible investment opportunity for many reasons. If you have the amount of time required to invest in it, as well as the finances available, getting started in real estate can be highly profitable. It offers many of the benefits that investors are looking for, and does not necessarily have to come at a high time-cost.

Precious Goods

One interesting way to invest is to purchase precious goods. Precious metals and other highly valuable items, such as vintage cars that have been maintained incredibly well, can actually be a wonderful investment. Not only are they typically cherished by their owner, but they also tend to hold a high value and can resell at an incredible price for the owner if they should ever desire to sell it.

The best way to make a profit through precious goods is to look for opportunities to purchase them at a lower price and then hold onto them while their value increases. With this tactic, the value increases over time. This means that you should only invest in precious goods if you intend on staying invested in them for a long-term growth opportunity. This is not a valuable short-term growth strategy. It may also be too risky for those who are planning to bank on them as their retirement fund, so be sure to have this as a secondary option if you truly want to invest but rely on the funds involved!

It is ideal to invest in these goods by using your extra money. For example, creating a secondary retirement investment strategy before proceeding. This would create the potential to significantly increase your profits so that you have even more when you are ready to retire. However, there's also the possibility that their value might fall and not earn you the profit you were hoping for.

The best way to invest in these goods is to find them on a sale or at auctions. However, if you are purchasing precious metals, you can also purchase them directly from dealers. Again, you want to purchase them in any situation where you can get them for the lowest price possible to maximize your overall profits.

Currency

Many people choose to invest in currency as an opportunity to hedge against inflation. An easy way to explain is this, imagine you purchased $1000 USD back when the United States Dollar was not performing as strongly as the Canadian Dollar. Then, when the United States Dollar swung back up in value and became stronger than the Canadian Dollar, you went ahead and purchased Canadian Dollars. If you continued doing this, your funds would significantly increase. This means that you would maximize your profitability simply by investing in currency.

You can easily do this yourself, or you can do it with the help of an investor. Alternatively, investing in currency is also something that you can do directly in the stock market. If you want to get involved with the stock market, you can get involved with currencies right there.

Currency investments are a great way to maximize your profits, but it takes quite some time to do it. They should not be relied on as a solitary or primary investment strategy. Instead, they should be a supplementary or additional strategy. Since sometimes it can take even longer than a decade, for the currency to swing back in the alternative direction, and it is certainly something that requires plenty of patience.

Chapter 5: Types of Investment Funds

The following types of investments are investment funds that you can get involved in. These are low maintenance and are wonderful for anyone looking for either short-term or long-term investment solutions. Each one has a unique set of benefits to it, though most of them generally work the same way. You provide money and someone else overlooks the rest. All you truly have to do is meet with your advisor on a scheduled basis, typically every 3-6 months, to ensure that your investments are still performing optimally and that your relevant goals are being met. In this chapter, we will have a look at these investment funds and what they mean for you.

Mutual Funds

Mutual funds are a type of fund that involves shareholders (you) investing their funds in a 'mutual' fund. That is where the name come from. The fund is then watched over by a professional management team and is typically traded in some way or another. These trades may involve real estate, the stock market, or other investment strategies. Then, when you are ready, you can draw on the fund.

It is important that you pay attention to what the terms of the funds are. While they don't tend to be a fixed-term investment, some do prefer that you keep your investments with the fund for a longer period of time. As such, they may require you to sign an agreement to do so. If you decide that you want to draw on your funds sooner, there is usually a high fee that you will have to pay. It is important to understand how much that fee is and to be as certain as you possibly can that those funds are easily capable of staying there long-term. While an unexpected situation may arise, the goal is not to need the funds until you've reached the maturity date.

You can easily get involved in mutual funds through an investor. Investment advisors are the easiest way to do so, as they are typically directly involved with the professional management team that is responsible for overlooking the funds. You can get in touch with one of these advisors independently, or through a bank. They tend to operate in a variety of financial institutions, so they are fairly easy to come by. Ideally, however, you want to pick an advisor who you can rely on for many things, so make sure that you like them!

Bonds

Bonds are like a loan that you give to the bank. They are a form of debt that the bank creates with you. As such, they work virtually the same as a loan would for you, only in the opposite direction. Instead of you borrowing money from the bank and paying them an interest fee, the bank borrows money from you and pays you an interest fee.

The money will either be loaned directly to the bank, or may be loaned to the government, a city, a company, or anyone else. Essentially, the entity will borrow the money and promise to pay you back, with regular interest payments involved. This is a very safe investment strategy for anyone who is planning to get involved with investments but wants to protect themselves against the many risks that tend to arise from making an investment.

While bonds can be made available directly, the easiest way to get involved with this particular type of investment is through your advisor once again. Your advisor will make the appropriate arrangements with your funds to get them into the bond and get your profits back in the future if necessary. Additionally, working together with an advisor and financial institution ensures that the entity borrowing the money has been checked. You want to make sure that they are genuine, or that they can actually pay back the promised funds. If you are doing this privately or independently, it is necessary that you also take the appropriate steps to ensure that your loan will be paid in full and that the person or entity that you are loaning it to will not default on the loan. Doing it privately can earn you a higher percentage, but it can also put you at a higher risk. It is completely your choice whether or not you are willing to take that risk, though it is not usually advised unless you can be absolutely sure that the entity will pay you back.

Bank Products

There are many bank products available to you that make it easy to increase your funds through investments. Many of these products rely on the basic structure of a mutual fund or a bond, though they are specialized to meet the needs of specific goals. The most common ones include short-term and long-term savings with no specific needs, as well as retirements savings, education savings, and other types of specific savings.

The benefit of going to a bank is that your entire account is overlooked by the bank and that you are not required to do much to keep it going. If you do it through your own bank, it can also be easy to access and watch over as it grows, as in many cases these will be visible directly from your online banking application.

However, investing in these funds is considered somewhat conservative. This means that you won't make as much money through banking products as you will through other services and products. Although they are still a valuable tool, they may be insufficient for some investors. If you are someone who wants to take more risks to make more profits, you might want to stay away from these options or keep them as secondary choices. If you are someone who prefers conservative risk, then this may be the perfect solution for you!

In order to discover exactly what solutions are available to you, the best thing you can do is to go to your bank. Often, they will sit down with you and discuss your goals and provide you with the solutions that best meet the needs of your goals. As previously mentioned, these solutions are tailored to the specifics such as education or retirement savings, meaning that they are specifically designed to benefit those goals and, therefore, everything is geared towards helping you reach them.

Insurance

Another type of investment you can invest in is insurance. While insurance will not increase your profits, it is considered an investment as it does protect you and your assets. There are many different types of insurance that you can consider depending on what your needs are. Below are a few of the basics that you should know about:

Life insurance

Life insurance is a form of insurance that protects your family. Should you pass away, your life insurance would be made available to your beneficiary or beneficiaries. This could then be used to pay off your mortgage, any outstanding debt you may have, your funeral, and anything else that may need to be paid off. Anything remaining would then be a small lump sum made available to your family for whatever they may want or need to do with it.

Life insurance is beneficial if you tend to carry around a lot of debt, don't have a large amount of savings put away for your family should you pass away, or want to otherwise ensure that your family does not have to carry your financial burdens should you pass away.

Critical Illness Insurance

Critical illness insurance is a form of insurance that is made available to you should you ever fall critically ill. This insurance typically pays out in the instance that you are too ill to work or do anything. Essentially, the funds are intended to be used to cover your monthly expenses as well as your medical expenses. This can be valuable if you want to make sure that both you and your family do not have to carry your financial burdens should you ever be afflicted by a terrible health condition.

Unemployment Insurance

If you ever become unemployed, unemployment insurance is necessary. Most employers automatically pay this for you. Self-employed individuals are required to pay this themselves. Unemployment insurance becomes available to you if you ever lose your job. This ensures that you can cover the cost of living until you can get a new job. It is valuable as you have something to fall back on should anything happen to your job.

Homeowners Insurance

Homeowners insurance is available to homeowners to ensure that if anything were to ever happen to their home, they would be protected. For example, if their home was burned down or robbed, their losses would be covered by the insurance company. This is essentially a sweeping asset insurance, as it covers your home and everything inside of it. Another form of home insurance exists for tenants, known as 'tenant's insurance.' This does not directly provide the property with insurance but instead insures the tenant. Then, should anything ever happen, the tenant is covered. For example, if their unit was the first to catch on fire in an apartment building, their insurance would cover them. Or, if their home was robbed, their items would be repurchased by the insurance company.

Other Types of Insurance

There are many other types of insurances that exist out there. Just to name a few, there are other kinds like car insurance or precious asset insurance which are both used to protect expensive assets that you own. Debt insurance is purchased to protect your debt should you default. For example, if you lost your job then your debt insurance would cover your minimum payment for a set period of time. There is also pet insurance, health insurance, dental insurance, and more.

Chapter 6: Understanding Stocks

Stocks are another really incredible investment opportunity for people to get involved in. If you want to get started on investing in the stock market, you can either do so directly or through an investment agency. If you do it directly, you will need to download the software required. Ideally, then, you would want to purchase a guidebook directly on that software so that you can maximize your earning potential. The stock market has a lot of ins and outs for people to learn about should they want to make a profit out of it. There is simply too much for me to cover in this book. However, if you are interested in the stock market and want to understand it better, then use the assistance of a broker and an account manager to oversee your stock market involvement, this chapter is for you!

The Stock Market, Is It for You?

The stock market is a highly volatile trading platform. Although it can make you a lot of money, it can cause you to lose a lot too. It is important that if you get involved in stocks that you refrain from investing any funds that are necessary or important to you. Instead, invest your extra funds. In doing so, you eliminate any unnecessary risks that can harm you, and won't have so much 'riding on' the investment.

Although the stock market is volatile, it has the potential to earn you an incredible amount of money. Many people have become millionaires thanks to the stock market, simply because they have learned how to use it effectively. If you are looking for the opportunity to earn an incredible profit, the stock market is a great place to start. You can either learn how to do it yourself and invest your own time in earning profits, or you can hire someone else. If you intend on doing it yourself, know that you are going to have to invest quite a bit of time to make sure you'll make a profit. Stocks are something that has to be watched regularly so you don't end up taking a major hit. If you decide to hire someone else, the next section will give you some information on how you can do that and what to look for.

Brokers and Account Managers

Brokers are the people responsible for helping others find their way in the stock market. They may be large, or small. Account managers are the individuals who work for the brokers and they're the ones who work with you directly. These two work together to ensure that once you are prepared, you won't have problems making your way through the stock market. In essence, all you have to do is find a reliable broker and account manager and set up an appointment with them. Assuming that you like their style, that they have impressed you, and that you feel confident with picking them, you can then agree to allow them to oversee your account and you can let them take over your stock management.

Ideally, there are a few things you should look out for to ensure that the assistance you're being given is actually helpful. First off, arming yourself with as much knowledge about the stock market as you can is important. Understand that when you invest in the stock market you can try the lower risk categories, however, there is no such thing as investments with no risk. If someone tells you otherwise, this could be a sign that they're not being completely honest with you. Do not believe them even if they say that there is virtually no risk. This alludes to the idea that you do not have to worry. While you do not necessarily have to keep on worrying, you should know that the stocks are volatile, and your advisor should be open and honest with you about this. However, they should also assert that their company has a lot of experience with handling stocks and that they know how to effectively manage your account to minimize your risk. That is a safe and positive word to hear from an advisor.

You also want to make sure that the advisor is professional, and that they understand your needs. If they do not seem like they have the time to hear you out, or if they do not understand your wants, even after you have explained it to them, then they may be working for their own interests instead of yours. While they are being paid for their job to manage your account, you want to make sure that they are managing your account in a way that guarantees you'll be the one who benefits in the end. That is how they stay in business. If they are managing your account for their own selfish purposes, you should not invest in them.

Lastly, in the appointment, you want to make sure that it is you who will set the expectations. Not only should your goals be clearly laid out, but you should also ensure that you and your advisor are both on the same page about how the investments will be made, and how all follow-ups will be done. In other words, you should have a clear idea as to when you will meet again to discuss growth and progress.

How Money Is Made

In the stock market, money is made specifically by buying low and selling high. However, there are a few different ways in which this is done. For those who are involved in incredibly fast stock markets, they typically get involved in what is called 'scalping.' This essentially means buying a large number of stocks and selling them as soon as they've gone up a few cents in value. As a result, they earn a few dollars at a time. The idea here is to buy a massive amount of stocks while you wait for a small amount of growth. This is incredibly time-consuming, but it does earn a fairly decent profit for those who use it.

The next type is called 'day trading.' These are usually the trades that opens when the stock market opens and closes when it closes. These trades are shorter in length but do not require a rapid response like scalping the market. A trade may take minutes or hours, but will always be closed by the end of the day.

The last type of stock market trading requires you to wait quite some time. In general, you invest in an account or stock that is considered to be conservative and you let your funds sit for a long period of time. Then, when you are ready to take your profits, you simply go ahead and sell the next time the market is on the uptrend. These types of investments are typically made in massive corporations or in currencies that are known to be on the general uptrend. Since the stock market itself is always on the uptrend, if you get involved with stocks that are less risky, you know that they will be easier for you to get involved in and stay in for a long period of time. A common situation where we see this is with cryptocurrencies, which we will discuss next.

A Note on Cryptocurrencies

Cryptocurrencies are traded like stocks in the stock market. They are, however, traded on their own market. That is unless you are investing in the company and not the currency. For example, if you invest in Bitcoin the company, you would invest in the regular stock market. But if you invested in Bitcoins the currency, you would invest in the special cryptocurrency market. Both have been known to be highly valuable ways of increasing your funds, and remain extremely popular in the modern market. Much like with trading your own stocks in general, however, there is far more to explain that can reasonably fit within this guide. So, it is important that you understand that if you want to get involved directly with the currencies themselves as opposed to the companies that own the currencies, you need to have a look at cryptocurrency-specific trading guides that can help you get started so you can earn high profits.

Conclusion

Thank you for reading *Investing for Beginners: The Only Money Guide You'll Ever Need.*

This guide was designed to arm you with the best knowledge and understanding the countless possibilities when it comes to investing. Investing is an incredibly powerful solution for maximizing your savings and increasing your earning potential. While it was once reserved for the elite and wealthy, it is now an incredibly necessary strategy for anyone who desires to have money long-term.

I hope that this book was able to equip you with enough knowledge so you can feel confident in investing your money. Knowing how valuable and important it is to invest, it is equally important that you feel confident in the act of investing itself. Knowing as much as you can about investing and different strategies will give you the wisdom to make the best decisions with your funds so you won't ever feel like you made an unwise decision based on a lack of education around the choice.

The next step is to take action on the goals you have defined for yourself. You can either do so directly or take the necessary action of hiring a financial advisor who can overlook your account and help you. Remember, even if you hire an advisor you still need to keep up to speed with the knowledge and the current state of financial affairs. The more knowledge you have, the better you can advocate for yourself in your advisor-to-client relationship and ensure that your exact needs and desires are being met.

Lastly, if you enjoyed *Investing for Beginners: The Only Money Guide You'll Ever Need*. I ask that you please take the time to review it. Your honest feedback would be greatly appreciated.

Thank you!

Did you know that a large percent of people who make a lot of money lose it within the first couple years?
It doesn't take much for a person to lose all of their money. Around 2 in 3 lottery winners lose all of their winnings within 5 years. If someone could lose hundreds of millions of dollars over a couple years, how fast will you lose your millions that you could make from this book?

Over the past couple years I have stumbled upon the key secret behind managing money and KEEPING it. If you follow the link below you will uncover the truth behind managing and keeping the money you make

>>> Click/Tap here to Learn the Secret Behind Money Management <<<

Or Go to https://secretstomoneymanagement.gr8.com/

Description

Investing for Beginners: The Only Money Guide You'll Ever Need is a powerful investment guide that was designed to help beginners get started in investing.

It is important to understand that investing is no longer a strategy that is reserved for the elite and wealthy. Instead, it is a smart and necessary strategy for anyone who desires to have any form of financial stability in their life.

Effectively investing your funds will help meet both your short-term and long-term goals with ease. Proper investments make sure that your money is always working for you and that you are not exposed to the ever-rising threat of inflation.

If you are new to the world of investing, *Investing for Beginners: The Only Money Guide You'll Ever Need* is a descriptive guide that will ensure that you are equipped with all of the knowledge you need to start out strong. As long as you are armed with valuable knowledge and understanding, you can be certain that you will become a strong investor and that you will surely reach your financial goals.

Just because anyone can get started on investing doesn't mean that just about anyone should do it. The only people who should truly get involved are those who are willing to educate themselves and maximize their profitability through knowledge and understanding. You can start now by reading, *Investing for Beginners: The Only Money Guide You'll Ever Need*. By the end, you will feel empowered to make smart choices with your investments so that you can become a powerful investor, too!

Bitcoin

Mastering Bitcoin for Starters

By Stephen Smith

financial, investment, tax, or legal adviser. This book should not be taken as financial or investment advice, and the author does not take any responsibility for inaccuracies, omissions, or errors. The author of this work is not responsible for any loss, damage, or inconvenience caused as a result of reliance on information as published on, or linked to, this book.

The author of this book has taken careful measures to share vital information about the subject. May its readers acquire the right knowledge, wisdom, inspiration, and succeed.

Introduction

Congratulations on downloading this book and thank you for doing so.

The following chapters will teach you the ins and outs of investing in bitcoin and how you can turn it into a goldmine of profits:

Chapter 1 lays down the basics to help you to have a good understanding of what bitcoin really is.

Chapter 2 gives an overview and teaches how you can get started with using bitcoin.

Chapter 3 discusses the blockchain technology which is the backbone technology of bitcoin. It also explains how a bitcoin transaction works.

Chapter 4 talks about the different types of bitcoin wallets.

Chapter 5 teaches how you can buy bitcoins.

Chapter 6 is about using bitcoin. Learn about receiving, sending, and receiving bitcoins.

Chapter 7 teaches effective strategies that you can use to invest in bitcoin.

Chapter 8 talks about businesses that use bitcoins, as well as how *you* can easily use it for your own business.

Chapter 9 is about bitcoin mining. Learn about the different ways to mine bitcoins.

Chapter 10 talks about the security of using bitcoin.

There are plenty of books on this subject on the market, thanks again for choosing this one! Every effort was made to ensure it is full of as much useful information as possible. Please enjoy!

Did you know that a large percent of people who make a lot of money lose it within the first couple years?
It doesn't take much for a person to lose all of their money. Around 2 in 3 lottery winners lose all of their winnings within 5 years. If someone could lose hundreds of millions of dollars over a couple years, how fast will you lose your millions that you could make from this book?

Over the past couple years I have stumbled upon the key secret behind managing money and KEEPING it. If you follow the link below you will uncover the truth behind managing and keeping the money you make

>>> Click/Tap here to Learn the Secret Behind Money Management <<<

Chapter 1: What is Bitcoin?

Bitcoin is undeniably the number one cryptocurrency in the world. What is a *cryptocurrency*? A cryptocurrency is a kind of digital asset that is held electronically. It is stored online; and therefore, it does not have a physical existence. Just like other cryptocurrencies, bitcoin functions as a substitute for money.

Bitcoin is a *decentralized* digital currency. It is decentralized in the sense that there is no government, organization, group, or person that exercises authority over it. This makes it free from any and all forms of manipulation and undue advantage. This is also why so many people trust bitcoin.

It should be noted that although cryptocurrencies like bitcoin work as a substitute for money, they are not considered as fiat money or legal tender. Fiat money refers to the established and official currency of a state such as the US dollar. Legal tender refers to "that which a debtor may compel a creditor to accept payment." Although bitcoin is not considered as fiat money or legal tender, it is noteworthy that many individuals and merchants these days now accept bitcoin as a medium of payment. In fact, among all the cryptocurrencies out there, bitcoin is the most accepted cryptocurrency. Just to give you an idea, the giant computer company, Microsoft, now accepts payments in bitcoins. Not only that, Virgin Galactic, a huge company engaged in space tourism, also accepts payments in bitcoins. Other known companies like Overstock, Fiverr, Steam, Peach Airlines, Lionsgate Films, and Stripe, among many others, accept and use bitcoins. As Bitcoin gets more and more popular in the market, the more people and businesses start to use it.

Brief History

In 2008, a paper was posted on a cryptography mailing list. It was entitled *Bitcoin: A Peer-to-Peer Electronic Cash System*. It was published under the name Satoshi Nakamoto, which turned out to be just a pseudonym. The following year, Bitcoin was finally launched in the market. It came into existence just after Nakamoto himself mined the very first bitcoin block known as the *genesis block*.

Back then, bitcoin did not have any significant value. In fact, so many people did not even realize how much bitcoin would grow. At that time, it was the members of the cryptocurrency community themselves who decided how much bitcoin would worth. For example, there was a famous transaction where two pizzas where bought for 10,000 bitcoins. This is still posted on the *bitcointalk* forum. As you can see, most of the people there did not take it seriously. If only they knew how much bitcoin would develop. As of January 16, 2018, the price of 1 bitcoin is around 13,500 USD.

Who is Satoshi Nakamoto?

When people talk about the creator of bitcoin, they are well aware that it was made by Satoshi Nakamoto. But, who exactly is Satoshi Nakamoto? The truth is that up to the present time, nobody knows the real identity of Satoshi Nakamoto. There are many different views about this: There are those who say that Nakamoto is actually composed of a group of computer experts and programmers, while others say that Nakamoto is even a woman. Another theory is that Satoshi Nakamoto is Hal Finney, the man who first downloaded the bitcoin software and received 10 bitcoins from Nakamoto simply for downloading it. However, when Mr. Finney was still alive, he had already denied this claim. It is also worth mentioning that *Satoshi* is also the smallest unit of bitcoin. Bitcoin has 8 decimal places. Example: $0.00000001 = 1$ satoshi. Simply put, no one knows for certain the true identity of Satoshi Nakamoto. Nakamoto has long withdrawn from the public that nobody even knows his whereabouts. However, even though nobody knows who the real Satoshi Nakamoto is, and even if his identity remains a mystery forever, the fruit of his labor and contribution to the world, bitcoin, has gained worldwide popularity and success.

Why Invest in Bitcoin?

It is not a secret that most people who engage in the cryptocurrency market and possess bitcoins do not really use such cryptocurrency as a mere medium of exchange. In fact, they view bitcoin as a form of investment. So, you must be thinking: *Just how much profit can I reasonably make?* To give you an idea, here is the classic example: If you had invested even just $500 in bitcoin in 2009 or even in 2010, then you would have already earned millions by now. Yes, this is how profitable investing in bitcoin can be. Unlike investing in stocks where an annual return of 30% is already considered very high, you can obviously earn so much more when you invest in bitcoin. Hence, many professional stock investors have started moving their investments from stocks into bitcoins. Another benefit of investing in bitcoin is that you do not have to wait for a year just to experience a significant price increase. It is not uncommon for the price of bitcoin to increase by more than 30% within a week. There was even a time when the price of bitcoin increased by $2,000 in just a week's time.

Investing in bitcoin is also easy and convenient. Since cryptocurrencies are held electronically online, all you need is Internet access to start investing, and you can manage your account and all your investments in the comfort of your home. In fact, you can even do all these directly from your mobile phone. Indeed, now is the time for you to enjoy the beauty of technology and the profitability of bitcoin.

Of course, just like any other investment, there is also a risk that you may not earn anything and that you may even lose your investment. However, there are strategies that you can do to prevent this from happening. By using the right strategies as revealed in this book, you can effectively increase your rate of success by more than 75%.

So, should you invest in bitcoin? Well, if you are the type who is afraid of taking risks, then perhaps this investment is not right for you.

However, if you are the type who wants to earn and enjoy a high amount of profit, if you are willing to take risks and spend time and effort to study the market, if you want a proven way to achieve financial freedom, then investing in bitcoin might just be the best investment decision that you can ever make.

High Volatility

When people talk about bitcoin, they usually say that it has a high volatility. This is true. But, what does it mean when you say that bitcoin has a *high volatility*? This means that the price of bitcoin changes rapidly and significantly. This explains why it is possible for you to earn more than 200% profit in just a few days. However, be careful about this since this also implies that it is also possible for the price of bitcoin to drop just as fast. This is a normal part of the risk of investing in bitcoin or any other cryptocurrency. The whole cryptocurrency market itself is simply highly volatile. However, do not let this discourage you. Just remember that it is exactly this high volatility nature of bitcoin that makes it a highly lucrative investment. The good news is that if you study the past and current trend of bitcoin, you can easily see that it is a very profitable investment. Indeed, the price of bitcoin as of the beginning of 2018 has been gradually decreasing. However, keep in mind that it first increased significantly. This is merely part of the usual fluctuations that you can expect in the market. The important thing is that, in the long run, the value of your investment should be growing. Bitcoin has well established itself for years, and nobody can deny that it is still the number one and most successful cryptocurrency in the market.

Be careful with your understanding of high volatility. Many people think that high volatility means that after a significant price increase, then the price will drop significantly afterward, and vice versa, as if it balancing the rise and fall of the price on its own. This is a wrong understanding of high volatility. Take note that bitcoin (as well as other cryptocurrencies) does not balance itself on its own. Instead, some factors affect its price, such as market competition, economy, technological developments, market acceptance, and government regulations, among many others. Hence, you need to consider all these factors when predicting whether the price of bitcoin will rise or fall, but rest assured that a cryptocurrency will not balance its price movements all by itself. This is also why you need to do research and analysis when you engage in the cryptocurrency market.

What are Altcoins?

When you read about bitcoin, you will definitely also encounter other cryptocurrencies like Ethereum, Litecoin, Ripple, Lisk, OmiseGO, and others. All of these are altcoins. Simply put, all cryptocurrencies are considered as altcoin except bitcoin. Bitcoin has established itself strongly in the market that it has become the leading standard of all cryptocurrencies, such that all other coins are merely called as *altcoins*, a term that is simply short for *alternative coins*. To date, there are already more than 1,000 altcoins that have been created. Still, among all the cryptocurrencies in the world, Bitcoin holds the number one position and is considered the top and most successful and popular cryptocurrency of all.

Anonymity

Bitcoin users enjoy a certain level of anonymity. This is because, in a bitcoin transaction, no personal details will be revealed. This is true even though bitcoin has a *public* blockchain. When you look at the bitcoin blockchain, you will only see a bitcoin wallet address of the sender and of the bitcoin wallet address of the recipient. You will also see the amount of bitcoins involved in the transaction, as well as a time stamp. However, the names and other sensitive information will remain confidential. What about the bitcoin wallet address? It is simply like a long string of random letters and numbers, and a bitcoin user can always request for a new wallet address for free with just a few clicks of a mouse. In fact, it is suggested that to minimize exposure, you should request for a new wallet address for every new transaction that you make.

On legal matters

Although bitcoin is decentralized in such a way that no central authority governs and controls it, it does not mean that states do not have the power to regulate its use within their jurisdiction. Due to the level of anonymity enjoyed by bitcoin users, it is not hard to understand why some states like Ecuador and Bolivia completely outlaw the use of bitcoins, as well as all other cryptocurrencies. Due to the nature of cryptocurrencies, they can easily be used in illegal activities like money laundering and tax evasion. The good news is that in many countries like in the U.S., Canada, Europe, Russia, South Korea, Singapore, Philippines, and so many others, the use of bitcoins and other cryptocurrencies is legal. Russia used to consider it as illegal but then it changed its position in 2017 and now also uses bitcoin. Over time, more and more states and businesses are being open to the use of bitcoin.

As a bitcoin investor, you should keep an eye on the latest government regulations on bitcoin and other cryptocurrencies. Although there are states that do not outlaw the use of bitcoin in their territories, it does not mean that they can no longer impose regulations on the use of bitcoin. As of recently, the price of bitcoin and other known cryptocurrencies have been experiencing a decline. According to the news, this is because of certain regulations imposed by various states. But, do not worry; this has always been expected to happen. This is just one of the fluctuations that you can expect in the market. Soon enough, things will get more stable, and you can expect the prices to increase again. One thing to remember is that legal matters, especially the regulations imposed by states, have a strong influence on the price of bitcoin, as well as other cryptocurrencies. For example, when a news piece was released stating that South Korea was considering shutting down all its cryptocurrency exchanges, the price of bitcoin and all other cryptocurrencies experienced a significant decrease in price. This is nothing new; back in 2017, China also made a similar declaration, and the price of bitcoin and altcoins also experienced a drop in price. Once again, the lesson here is to consider how governments react to the use of cryptocurrencies, especially with regard to their legalities.

Chapter 2: Getting Started with Bitcoin

Now that you have a good idea of what bitcoin is, it is time for you to have an overview of how to get started with bitcoin so that you will know just what to expect. Well, the first step is to create a bitcoin wallet. There are basically just two types of bitcoin wallets: The hot and cold wallet. However, they are further divided into more specific types. Do not worry; they will be discussed in detail later on in this book. For now, you should learn what hot and cold wallets are.

Simply put, a hot wallet is a kind of bitcoin wallet that is stored completely online. As such, it is very easy and convenient to use. Hence, most cryptocurrency users use a hot wallet. All that you need to do is to sign up for an account for free from a wallet provider like *Coinbase*. The signing up process usually takes less than two minutes to complete. After which, you can now start using your bitcoin wallet. A cold wallet is the kind of bitcoin wallet where you store your private and public keys *offline*. Hence, to access your wallet and transfer funds, you will need to have your cold wallet in your possession. This is an added and highly effective security measure.

The next step is for you to own bitcoins. After all, the only way to invest and take advantage of bitcoin is by having bitcoins of your own. Although there are different ways to earn bitcoins, the quickest and fastest way to earn a good amount of bitcoins is by buying them. Bitcoin wallets like Coinbase will allow you to buy (and even sell) bitcoins directly from the wallet itself. This makes things very convenient for you. However, if the wallet that you use does not allow you to buy bitcoins, then you can simply sign up for a trading account with a cryptocurrency trading broker. Again, creating an account is also fast and simple. However, it is important that you only work with a reliable and trusted broker. When you search online, you will surely find different brokers. As an investor, it is important that you only work with a reliable broker, so be sure to check the latest ratings and reviews of a broker prior to making any form of deposit.

Once you have bitcoins of your own, then you can keep them, and then sell them at a profit once they appreciate in value. However, the activity of investing in bitcoin is much more technical than just buying and selling bitcoin. After all, how do you know the right time to buy and sell bitcoin? Do not worry; all these will be discussed later in the book. For now, it is important for you to just have an idea of how you will get started.

As a bitcoin investor, you should know that research and analysis should be part of your day-to-day activity as an investor. Hence, before you even start to actually use and invest in bitcoin, you should already begin reading about the cryptocurrency market by now. Take note that bitcoin has many other competitors. Therefore, even though you may only intend to invest in bitcoin, it is still important that you keep an eye on its competitors, such as Ethereum, Litecoin, Ripple, Dash, and others. And, who knows, you might even be able to discover other profitable investment opportunities in the process.

Chapter 3: Understanding Blockchain and Bitcoin Transactions

Before we discuss the specific steps on how you can profit by investing in bitcoin, you should first understand the technology behind bitcoin. Take note that the backbone technology of bitcoin is known as the *blockchain technology* or simply *blockchain*. What is blockchain? It is a public and decentralized distributed ledger which also acts as a repository of all transactions. It is made of records referred to as blocks. Before any block is added to the chain, it will undergo a strict process of verification and confirmation, which ensures that all the records that will be added to the chain are true and correct. Every new block is connected to the block that comes before it using what is known as a *hash pointer*. This way, all of the blocks in the blockchain network are interconnected with one another.

The blockchain is decentralized, which means that no organization exercises authority over it. It functions on its own free from any and all forms of influence and manipulation. This is why many people trust this system since there is no need for human intervention and control. The blockchain is also public, which means that all of the transactions are viewable to everyone on the network. This gives it added transparency and fairness and ensures that all transactions are legitimate and correct.

The blockchain technology is also an effective preventive measure against double spending and fraud, which are common problems in financial circles. When you use blockchain, there is absolutely no way to withdraw, modify, or cancel a transaction after it is confirmed. Not even Satoshi Nakamoto himself can stop or change it.

It also has a high level of security. Keep in mind that the blockchain network is spread over a wide connection of computers. For an attack against the blockchain system to be successful, the said attack has to possess at least 51% of the total hash rate of the entire bitcoin blockchain. Since the network is spread over a vast number of computers, achieving the said 51% can be considered as impossible. Take note that an attack with less than 51% hash rate is still possible, but you simply cannot expect for it to be successful. This is the idea behind the 51% attack concept.

It is noteworthy that bitcoin is not the only one that is gaining lots of attention and popularity. The blockchain technology has been making a name for itself apart from it being associated with bitcoin and other cryptocurrencies. This is because the blockchain has many other possible applications that are even well beyond the financial sector. Still, it can be said that blockchain is still a fairly new and young technology. Hence, there is still a room for improvement, and it is definitely something to keep an eye on.

How a Bitcoin Transaction Works

Every bitcoin transaction goes through a process. You should remember that there are 3 parts of a bitcoin transaction: Input, Output, and the Amount. Let us take a look at them one by one:

✓ Input

Let us say that person A wants to send 2 bitcoins to person B. Before person A can send B 2 bitcoins, it is only logical that person A must first have 2 bitcoins in his wallet. This is what is referred to as the *input*. Simply put, it refers to the bitcoins in the sender's wallet, the amount of which should be greater than or at least equal to the amount that he wants to send to another.

✓ Output

The output refers to the receiver. In our example, it is person B. More specifically, it refers to the *wallet address* of person B. Take note that in a bitcoin transaction, you do not send the bitcoin directly to the name of the receiver. In a blockchain, the transfer of bitcoins is made between wallet addresses. Hence, if you are the sender, then you should first ask for the bitcoin wallet address of the receiver. It is to this wallet address where you will send bitcoins.

✓   Amount

Obviously, this refers to the amount that is involved in a transaction. In this case, the amount is 2 bitcoins.

What about mining?

Mining refers to the process of verifying, confirming, and adding blocks or records to the blockchain. In a bitcoin transaction, once miners confirm a transaction, it can no longer be canceled, withdrawn, or modified. As you can see, mining is an important part of the blockchain ecosystem. Without mining, no new block or record can be added to the blockchain. Hence, in a bitcoin blockchain, you can rest assured that there is always a demand for miners.

Chapter 4: Where to Keep Your Bitcoin

Now, let us move on to the more practical side: Do you keep or store your bitcoins? Remember that there are two kinds of bitcoin wallets: the hot and cold wallet. Now, these two main categories of bitcoin wallets are further classified into several specific types. You need to understand their differences so that you will know which wallet type will best suit your needs. Let us look at them one by one:

- Online Wallet

An online wallet is the most common type of bitcoin wallet. It is also known as a *web wallet*. This is the most commonly used type of bitcoin wallet as it is very easy and convenient to use. Good examples of an online wallet are Coinbase and GreenAddress. This is the type of wallet that you can easily access and manage simply by going online and logging in to your wallet through the site provided by your wallet provider. However, take note that this is a hot wallet, so you cannot expect for it to be a secured as a cold wallet. The good news is that many of the reputable hot wallets have already updated their security features. But, if security is your main concern, then a cold wallet is still the best choice.

- Mobile Wallet

A mobile wallet is another type of hot wallet. It is also an online wallet; but this time, you should download the wallet application on your mobile phone. Normally, you can download the application for free at the Apple and/or GooglePlay store. Many people use their phones to access the Internet, so having a mobile version of your wallet can be really handy at times. Do not worry; many web wallets like GreenAddress and Coinbase also have a mobile version of their bitcoin wallet.

- Desktop Wallet

A desktop wallet is a type of cold wallet. When you use a desktop wallet, you will store your public and private keys on a computer, which may also be a laptop computer. Before you use any computer as a desktop wallet, you should first reformat your computer or at least ensure that it is free from any malware and virus. Also, once you start using a computer as a cold wallet, you should no longer connect it to the Internet. This is what makes a cold wallet more secure than a hot wallet. Once something is exposed to the Internet, then it gets exposed to online hazards like hackers, attackers, and viruses. Since cold wallets are held offline, they are free from such risks. This is what makes a desktop wallet and other cold wallets very secured.

- Hardware Wallet

A hardware wallet functions just like a desktop wallet. But, instead of storing your public and private keys in a computer, you get to store them in a hardware. Although you can use an ordinary USB for this purpose, such is not advisable since an ordinary USB does not have enough protective features and can get easily get corrupted. Different kinds of hardware wallets are sold in the market specially made for this purpose, such as the Ledger Nano. However, they can get expensive. The good news is that to date, there has been no report or issue of any hardware wallet getting hacked or compromised. Hence, this is definitely one of the best bitcoin wallets that you can use in terms of having a very high level of security.

- Paper Wallet

A paper wallet is another famous type of cold wallet. When you use a paper wallet, you get to store your private and public keys on a paper. You can print them on paper. Ideally, you should keep several copies. Needless to say, you should store them in a safe place where they will not be stolen. Take note that although cold wallets offer high security, this is only as far as online hazards are concerned. They still cannot protect you from thieves or from losing or breaking your cold wallet.

Which wallet type should you use?

When choosing the right wallet for you, you need to strike a balance between security and convenience. For convenience, then any of the hot wallets would be a good choice. If you want to focus more on security, then you should use a cold wallet.

When choosing a wallet, you should think about how you intend to use your bitcoins. If you know that you will most likely transact with bitcoins on a regular basis, then you should use a hot wallet. However, if you just want to make a long-term investment where you just want to keep your bitcoins for a period of time, then using a cold wallet would be a better choice.

You are also free to use several wallet types at the same time. Hence, you can have a cold wallet and a hot wallet at the same time. You can use a hot wallet for short-term investments and for your day-to-day transactions, and then you can use a cold wallet at the same time for your long-term investment in bitcoin. There are also professional bitcoin investors who use multiple hot and cold wallets at the same time. You may find this necessary once you have a high number of bitcoins. After all, it is not advisable to keep all your bitcoins in a single wallet despite how secured you believe it to be. As they say, "Do not put all your eggs in one basket." The same is true when it comes to storing and keeping your bitcoins.

Chapter 5: Buying Bitcoin

How do you buy bitcoins? Buying bitcoins is easy. In fact, there are hot wallets like Coinbase and coins.ph will allow you to purchase bitcoins directly from the wallet itself. Now, if this is not possible, then you can sign up for a trading account with a cryptocurrency trading broker. There are brokers like eToro that will allow you to deposit fiat money and buy bitcoins on the trading platform itself. You may also want to use *localbitcoins*. It is like a marketplace where people buy and sell bitcoins. However, you need to be cautious when you use such kind of cryptocurrency marketplace as there are many scammers out there. Another popular option is to buy bitcoins using PayPal by through Virwox. However, take note that this is not a suggested approach as the cost can get very expensive. Hence, there are only two suggested ways to buy bitcoins: Through your bitcoin wallet and a trustworthy cryptocurrency trading broker.

Buy price vs. Sell price

Before you purchase bitcoins, you first need to understand that there is a difference between the buy price and the sell price. The buy price is always higher than the sell price. This difference in price is how a broker or seller makes a profit. This also means that right after you buy bitcoins, you cannot just sell them immediately after their price fluctuates a little higher as you will most probably end up with a loss since the sell price will be lower than the price at which you bought your bitcoins. Be sure to keep this in mind both when selling and buying bitcoins.

Check the market price

Before you buy and sell bitcoins, be sure to check its current price in the market. Do not forget that the price of Bitcoin fluctuates rapidly. This is to ensure that you are buying/selling your bitcoins at a fair price. A good way to do this is to visit the site of well-known cryptocurrency traders like Bitfinex, Binance, and Bittrex. You can also check well-established websites that share information about the cryptocurrency market, such as *coinmarketcap* and *coingecko*.

Timing

Do not just buy bitcoins right away. Before you make a purchase, you should first study the cryptocurrency market. Do not forget that bitcoin has a high volatility and that its price continuously changes. You definitely would not want to buy bitcoin when its price is falling down. Therefore, it is important that you study the market and use proper timing. Take note that the price of bitcoin rises and falls; hence, you may have to enter (buy) and leave (sell) the market every now and then, depending on the circumstances. By taking the effort to study the market, you will be able to save yourself some money and even lower your expenses and losses. Keep in mind that you do not just enter the market at any time you want. You need to be objective about it, and only buy bitcoins if you think that now is the moment to make a profitable investment. It is not uncommon for professional investors to wait for a day or even a week before they purchase bitcoins, even though they are eager to invest. Once again, proper timing is important when buying, as well as when selling bitcoins.

When selling bitcoins, you would want to sell them when their price is about to fall. However, this may also depend on your strategy. If you are making a long-term investment, then you should expect to face various price fluctuations in the market, and this includes facing some price decreases. Do not worry; in a long-term investment, the only important thing is to be at a profit once you close your position (when you sell your bitcoins). Hence, even if the price falls by 30% after two weeks, it would not matter if you can profit, say, by 100% the following week or so. Of course, you would not be investing blindly. To turn the odds in your favor and significantly increase your chances of making a profit, you will have to use effective strategies (as discussed later in this book).

Chapter 6: Using Bitcoin

Using bitcoin is very easy and convenient. As we have already discussed, many merchants accept payments in bitcoin. Today, there are also many people around the world who use bitcoins for remittance or for sending funds to people located in another country. Since the use of bitcoin effectively cuts away the middleman like banks, it is a good way to minimize your cost. Now let us discuss what you need to do when you use bitcoins:

✓   Sending bitcoins

If you are the one who will send bitcoins, then all you need to do is ask for the bitcoin wallet address of the person to whom you intend to send bitcoins. A bitcoin wallet address looks like a long string of random letters and numbers. Be sure to copy and paste it correctly. Do not forget that once a transaction is confirmed, there is no way that you can cancel, amend, withdraw it. Therefore, be very careful when sending bitcoins. Be sure that you send it to the correct bitcoin wallet address. To send bitcoins, just access your wallet, key in the amount that you want to send, and then paste the wallet address of the recipient, and just click *send*. This entire process can be completed in less than a minute. As you can see, it is very simple. The recipient will soon be notified in his wallet that there is a pending receivable. Once the transaction has passed through several confirmations, then he will be able to finally receive the bitcoins that you send to his account. This normally takes just a few minutes from the time of sending the bitcoins.

✓   Receiving bitcoins

If you are the recipient, then you simply have to give your bitcoin wallet address to the sender. Again, to avoid committing mistakes, you should simply copy and paste your wallet address when sharing it with the sender.

✓   Storing bitcoins

We have already discussed the different ways to store your bitcoins. Make sure to keep your bitcoin wallet safe and secured. There are certain strongly suggested practices that you should observe, such as using a strong password and allowing the two-factor authentication. Keep in mind that your bitcoin wallet password is your main line of defense against a hacker or anyone who would want to access your account without your consent. To have a strong password, you should combine both upper and lower case letter. You should also use numbers and symbols in your password. Last but not least, avoid simply using the minimum required a number of characters. Instead, use a long password of at least 15 characters long. Needless to say, do not use a password that other people can easily guess. The two-factor authenticator is another line of defense that your account has. When you enable it, a code will be sent to your phone when anyone tries to access your account. Normally, you will have to enter this code after entering your password. The code changes within a few seconds, so it is very hard to predict correctly. You may have to download Google Authenticator app to be able to view the code. Do not worry; you can easily download this application for free from the GooglePlay or Apple store. If you are using a cold wallet, be sure to keep it in a safe place where it will not be broken or stolen.

Chapter 7: Investing in Bitcoin

Investing in bitcoin follows the usual trader's maxim: Buy low, sell high. However, this is easier said than done. To be able to invest successfully in bitcoin, you need to use effective strategies. Here are some notable strategies that you should learn and practice:

➢ Fundamental Analysis

Fundamental analysis is probably the most important strategy that you should learn. It is also referred as the lifeblood of investment. When you use fundamental analysis, you should focus on the *basics* or the fundamentals that affect bitcoin. Therefore, you should follow on the news and be up-to-date with the latest developments. The key to using this strategy is to gather as much good-quality information as you can. As they say, "Knowledge is power." It is a basic rule in investing that the more that you know and understand a certain asset, the more likely that you will be able to predict its price movement in the market. The same applies when you invest in bitcoin or any other cryptocurrency. When you use fundamental analysis, you should research and analyze the news, economy, competition among the different cryptocurrencies, market acceptance, and the past and current trend of bitcoin, among many others. Indeed, fundamental analysis is probably the strategy that takes a lot of effort, but it is well worth it. In fact, if you are serious about being a professional bitcoin investor, then it is a must that you should learn and use fundamental analysis. After all, this strategy can easily be incorporated even when you are using another strategy.

It is also strongly suggested that you should join online groups and forums about bitcoin and other cryptocurrencies. This is a good way to gather more information. From time to time, you will definitely learn some interesting ideas and strategies from these groups and forums. Since you are investing in bitcoin, be sure to join and participate in the *bitcointalk* forum. If you do not want to participate, then at least read the posts and learn something from them. It is also worth mentioning that many cryptocurrency developers are active in such kind of forums and groups, and this can allow you to gain valuable information against the competitors of bitcoin. Indeed, if you are serious about making continuous profit y investing in bitcoin or any other cryptocurrency, fundamental analysis is the strategy that you should always use.

➢ Technical Analysis

Technical analysis is a favorite among many bitcoin investors. This strategy is good if you are more of a visual person who loves to study and analyze graphs. When you use technical analysis, you will be looking at graphs and charts that reflect the price movements of bitcoin. The idea behind this strategy is that all of the elements or factors that affect the price of bitcoin can be summed up and have their final effect on the price. Therefore, this goes to show that simply by dealing with the price movements of bitcoin, you also get to deal with the many factors and elements that affect bitcoin. Of course, the advantage of using this approach is that it is much simpler than fundamental analysis where you need to research, read, and analyze so many pieces of information and even involves computations (numbers). When you use technical analysis, the key is to be able to identify and take advantage of patterns. Yes, patterns do exist. However, they also come and go. Therefore, do not expect to see a pattern every time that you look at a graph or chart. A common mistake is to force to see a pattern even when there is actually no pattern to be seen. So, if you do not see a pattern, accept that it is not there and do not force an investment.

Technical analysis is a good strategy for short-term investments, while fundamental analysis is usually the choice when it comes to making long-term investments. Still, technical analysis is something that you can easily incorporate regardless of the strategy that you are using. After all, you simply have to view a chart or graph. Your trading broker will usually provide you with such tools (charts) that you need. If you do not have a trading broker, then there are many websites online that you can visit to see the price movements of bitcoin (as well as other cryptocurrencies).

Although you can use and depend completely on technical analysis, real experts suggest that you should still make use of fundamental analysis. The problem with technical analysis is that it does not give you the reasons behind the price movements; hence, you can barely come up with an accurate prediction. The best way to use technical analysis is still to combine it with fundamental analysis. If you use both strategies together properly, you can significantly increase your chances of making a profitable investment.

➢ Averaging Down

This is a good strategy to use if you want to be able to make a high amount of profit from an investment. This will allow you to purchase bitcoin at a "bargain" price. Here is an example of how to use this strategy: Let us say, for example, that the current price of bitcoin is $10,000. The first step is to make a buy order at its current price. Hence, you should buy bitcoin at the said price of $10,000. Now, if the price of bitcoin increases, then you make a profit. However, if the price of bitcoin drops, say, down to $9,500, then you should make another buy order at the said lower amount of $9,500. Now, if the price decreases again, then you should make another buy order. The key is simply to keep buying it while its price in decreasing. Hence, you get to buy bitcoin at a "bargain."

Okay, so this may seem like as if you are merely purchasing a losing asset, but this is actually not the case. Just imagine how much you will profit once the price of bitcoin recovers and goes back to its original price (the price when you first used this strategy), or even higher. All the buy orders that you have made will experience a nice profit. This is also an excellent strategy to use to take advantage of the volatility of the market.

Although this strategy is very practical and effective, do not forget that it is still considered an aggressive strategy. Hence, you should be careful when you use this approach. The proper way of using this strategy is to research the market first. Only use this strategy if you think that the price of bitcoin will most likely increase in the near future. If after doing your research and analysis, there are good reasons to believe that the price of bitcoin will most likely increase, then that is the only time that you should use this strategy.

➢   Quick Sell

This strategy is a good way to earn small yet consistent profits. The key to using this strategy is not to be greedy and close your position before your risk of exposure gets high. Here is an example of how you should use this strategy. Let us assume that the price of bitcoin is worth $10,000. You make a buy order at its current price of $10,000. Now, if the price increases, say, up to $10,200, then you should make a sell order right away and enjoy the small return of profits. Again, this is a good way to take advantage of a volatile market.

Take note, however, that the sell price is much lower than the buy price. Be sure to check the prevailing rate and only sell your bitcoin if you can make a profit out of it.

When you use this strategy, you should first study the market, especially the current trend of bitcoin. The best time to apply this strategy is while the price of bitcoin is increasing. Enter the market when it is hot and leave it even when it still appears to be profitable. The longer that you hold your position, the greater is your exposure to risk. Do not forget that when you use this strategy, you should prioritize controlling your risk. Hence, be contented with a small profit, and then start over.

➢   Wait It Out

There are times when it can be difficult to invest in bitcoin. For example, as of the start of 2018, the price of bitcoin has been unstable. This does not mean that it is no longer a good investment. Rather, this only shows that it may not be a good time to invest in bitcoin at the moment. Again, this is part of the usual fluctuations that you can expect when you deal with any kind of cryptocurrency/ however, you can rest assured that this will soon change (which is part of the nature of the cryptocurrency market). So, do not be like the other investors who keep on investing even when the market is down. To minimize your risk and losses, you should only invest in bitcoin when it is profitable in the market. But, when you see that its price has constantly been falling for days and weeks, the best action would be to just be patient and keep watch. Soon, bitcoin will again be able to recover, and that is the time for you to invest as its price continues to increase.

Remember that no matter how eager you are to invest in bitcoin, you must be patient to wait for the right opportunity. The important thing is that you are ready to invest once that opportunity arises. Therefore, it is your job to continue to follow and study the market. Wait out the bad times and join the hot streaks. Pay close attention to the market.

➤ Go with the Flow

Bitcoin is not really that hard to predict. For example, when it was announced in the news that China would close down all its local cryptocurrency exchanges, bitcoin and altcoins experienced a drop in price. However, when the news featured that Russia started to legalize bitcoins, the price of bitcoin surged upwards. The same is true when bitcoin was featured on CNN showing just how profitable an investment it is. Again, when Singapore declared that it would not issue any restriction yet on bitcoin, the price of bitcoin also increased. As you can see, sometimes you just have to go with the flow, and you can easily make a profit. Bitcoin is not always hard to predict. In fact, most of the time, it is very easy to predict the direction that its price movement will take in the market.

When you go with the flow, it is still advised that you do your fundamental analysis to be sure that you are not being misdirected. Sometimes what you read online or see in the news can be deceiving, especially when there is a pump and dump scheme. What is a pump and dump scheme? This fraudulent scheme is nothing new. In fact, it has been used in the stock market for years and is now being used in the cryptocurrency market. In a pump and dump scheme, a group of people will promote a certain cryptocurrency using some form of promotional hype. Their objective is to draw as much as positive attention and interest as possible to drive the price of the promoted cryptocurrency higher. However, once its price increases as other investors continue to make investments thinking that it is a profitable cryptocurrency, the people behind the scheme will then sell the cryptocurrency being promoted at a nice profit. The final result is that those behind the scheme can make a good profit while the investors (victims of the scheme) will be holding a losing asset. Hence, for you not to fall victim to this scheme, be sure to do your own analysis of the market and do not just follow the flow without doing any research.

Chapter 8: Bitcoin for Business

Businesses around the world also use Bitcoin. In fact, by using bitcoin in business, you can effectively cut down your cost as you would no longer need a middleman like banks and other financial sectors for sending and receiving money (cryptocurrency) to another. You have full control of everything. The process, as we have already discussed, is also very quick and simple. Indeed, many businesses use and accept bitcoins. Let us look at some of these known businesses that use bitcoin:

- Microsoft

Microsoft needs no introduction. This computer giant is known worldwide, and now it is also known for accepting payments in bitcoin when you buy from Windows or Xbox store.

- Virgin Galactic

This company engaged in space travel also accepts bitcoin. So, if you have lots of bitcoins in your possession, you can now buy your trip to space. The founder of Virgin Galactic openly admitted that he supports bitcoin cryptocurrency.

- Wikipedia

As you know, Wikipedia is a huge website where you can get tons of valuable information for free. Anyone who uses the Internet is familiar with Wikipedia. Well, although you can use Wikipedia for free, it is also known for accepting donations in bitcoin.

- Tesla

If you are interested in science and technology, perhaps you would also find it interesting to know that the company, Tesla, also uses and accepts payment in bitcoin. In fact, some of its inventions were funded using bitcoins.

- Peach Airlines

The Japanese airline known as Peach Airline also accepts payment in bitcoin. So, if you want to travel to another country and would love to pay for your airfare using bitcoins, you might want to buy your ticket from Peach Airlines

- Steam

Steam is a popular gaming platform with millions of registered and active users. You can now buy games and upgrades using bitcoins.

- Overstock

This company allows you to purchase big-ticket items. You can now buy products from Overstock using bitcoins. In fact, they have even partnered with a famous bitcoin wallet known as *Coinbase*.

Many other companies and businesses use and accept payments in bitcoin. Now, if you own a business, you can also take advantage of bitcoins by paying your employees in bitcoins. Just be sure to check if this is allowed in the laws of your country. Also, if your business normally involves sending and receiving funds, then you should really consider using bitcoins as it can effectively lower your expenses and will allow you to have complete control of the process. It is also good to use bitcoins if you are to send "money" to someone who is located in another country. The bitcoin system is open 24 hours a day every day; hence, you can easily send and receive bitcoins with just a few clicks of a mouse. If you are the recipient, then simply give your bitcoin wallet address to the sender, and just wait for him to send your bitcoins into your wallet.

Chapter 9: Bitcoin mining

Mining bitcoins is another investment that you might want to consider. As we have already discussed, there is always a demand for miners in the bitcoin blockchain; otherwise, there is no way for any record or transaction to be added to the chain and be completed. Now, there are different ways to mine bitcoins. Let us go over them one by one:

- Computer mining

This is the most basic way to mine for bitcoins. This is where you use your own computer for mining. You can do this by downloading GUIMiner and joining a mining pool. The suggested pool is the Slush's pool. However, this is only a good method to give you an experience of mining, but it is not a recommended method if you want to earn a decent amount of bitcoins. The reason is that a computer alone does not have sufficient hash power to mine a decent amount of bitcoins. You will most probably end up with more expenses on electricity than the actual amount of bitcoin that you could mine. Also, when you mine using your own computer, you will have to worry about overheating. Take note of this because this can break your computer's CPU. So, when it comes to earning a decent amount of bitcoins, this is not a recommended method. But, if you just want to experience how it feels like to mine bitcoins and earn a little, then this is a good start.

- Hardware mining

Since a computer alone is not enough to mine a decent amount of bitcoins due to its low mining power, you will have to use a mining hardware to increase your hash or mining power. There are websites online like Amazon and eBay where you can buy a mining hardware. It is noteworthy that even if you mine using a hardware, you still have to use your computer. Hence, you should still be careful about any overheating issues. You should follow a schedule that will allow your computer and mining hardware to cool down from time to time. In choosing a hardware, you should look at the mining power and also the electric consumption. It is not uncommon to find a strong mining hardware but then also consumes high electricity. You need to consider this to ensure that you will end up with a decent positive profit.

- Could mining

This seems to be the most famous method of mining bitcoins nowadays. With cloud mining, you no longer have to worry about any overheating issue. You do not even have to purchase any mining hardware. In fact, you do not even have to mine anything at all. Hence, you do not even have to use your computer. Instead, all that you need to do is to wait for the cloud mining company to send you bitcoins. You will usually receive your bitcoins every week or as soon as you meet the minimum threshold. Okay, this may sound too good to be true, so what is the catch? Of course, there is also a catch. After all, you cannot expect for any business to send you bitcoins every week just out of kindness. The catch is that you will first have to invest. This means that you must first pay a cloud mining company. Now, you have to be careful about this because there are many scammers online who simply want to rip you off of your money. Therefore, before you invest in any cloud mining company, you need to do your research, check the latest reviews given to the mining company, and learn as much as you can about the said company.

A usual offer may look something like this: Invest (or pay) 1 bitcoin and earn up to 0.035 bitcoins every week. Okay, so far this seems very ideal. You just have to make some simple computation, and you would already know when you can recover your investment, and then you can earn positive profits after that. However, this is not always the case. The problem is that the offer only shows the *expected* return and not the actual return of profits. This means that using the given example, you may receive less than 0.035 every week. Before you make any form of deposit or investment, you need to be sure that the terms and agreements of the contract are clear to you. In case of doubts, do not hesitate the customer support team, and they would be happy to assist you. Also, pay attention to the expiration date. There are cloud mining companies that only render the contract valid for a year — and so this means that you should be able to recover your investment and then earn profits within the same time period. Other cloud mining companies honor a lifetime validity of contract. Again, the best way to be sure about this is to read the contract and talk with the customer support team of the cloud mining company for clarifications.

Chapter 10: Security of Bitcoin

So, is it safe and secure to use bitcoin? The answer is *yes*. Otherwise, companies would no longer be using it in business. Although there were reports in the past that certain bitcoin wallets had been hacked, it is worth noting that the security of both hot and cold wallets has already improved significantly. In fact, many professional investors these days only use a hot wallet or the trading account provided by their cryptocurrency trading broker. The point here is that in terms of security, you can rest assured that bitcoin has a high level of security. Also, do not forget the 51% attack concept. Today, bitcoin is well distributed over a very vast network of computers, so just imagine how much hash rate power an attacker needs to have to penetrate the bitcoin blockchain successfully.

As an investor, you no longer need to worry whether or not bitcoin is secure because it is. Your main concern is how to ensure the security of your bitcoin wallet. As we have already discussed, you may want to use a cold wallet for this purpose. If you are using a hot wallet, be sure to enhance the security of your wallet by using a strong password and also activate the two-factor authentication or any other security features that your wallet provider may offer.

Bitcoin is also a continuously evolving technology, so you can expect for its security features to get even stronger and more secure over time. The good news is that as far as security is concerned, it can now be said that bitcoin is very secure. Hence, so many individuals and known businesses are using it, and many are still eager to learn about it so that they can also take advantage of the benefits of using bitcoin. In fact, there are those who believe that bitcoin is even more secure than traditional banks. As bitcoin continues to grow and dominate the cryptocurrency market, you can expect for more developments and improvements to happen over time.

Conclusion

Thanks for making it through to the end of this book. We hope it was informative and able to provide you with all of the tools you need to achieve your goals whatever they may be.

The next step is to apply everything that you have learned and start earning serious profits. Unfortunately, many people still think that bitcoin is a bubble that is about to burst. Well, it is up to you whether or not you want to believe this heresy. However, as far as the truth is concerned, those who believe that bitcoin is just a bubble failed to make any profit from it, while those who have taken the risk and believe in bitcoin as a profitable investment can earn a high amount of profits, even their way to complete financial freedom.

Finally, if you found this book useful in anyway, a review on Amazon is always appreciated!
Did you know that a large percent of people who make a lot of money lose it within the first couple years?

It doesn't take much for a person to lose all of their money. Around 2 in 3 lottery winners lose all of their winnings within 5 years. If someone could lose hundreds of millions of dollars over a couple years, how fast will you lose your millions that you could make from this book

Over the past couple years I have stumbled upon the key secret behind managing money and KEEPING it. If you follow the link below you will uncover the truth behind managing and keeping the money you make

>>> Click/Tap here to Learn the Secret Behind Money Management <<<

Description

Bitcoin: Mastering Bitcoin for Starters is the ultimate guide that will teach you how to master the number one cryptocurrency in the world, Bitcoin. Learn the ins and outs of Bitcoin, as well as how you can turn it into a highly profitable investment. This book unveils the secrets that will help you master Bitcoin.

Learn:

- ✓ What Bitcoin is
- ✓ What a cryptocurrency is
- ✓ History of bitcoin
- ✓ Blockchain technology
- ✓ How a Bitcoin transaction works
- ✓ The different types of bitcoin wallets
- ✓ Businesses that use and accept bitcoins
- ✓ Effective and powerful investing strategies
- ✓ Different ways to mine bitcoins
- ✓ Bitcoin security

And so much more!